ON ARRIVAL

ON ARRIVAL

1981–1995

Paul Rossiter

ISOBAR
PRESS

First published in 2019 by

Isobar Press
Sakura 2-21-23-202, Setagaya-ku,
Tokyo 156-0053, Japan

&

14 Isokon Flats, Lawn Road,
London NW3 2XD, United Kingdom

https://isobarpress.com

ISBN 978-4-907359-28-7

ACKNOWLEDGEMENTS

Grateful thanks to the editors of NOON: *journal of the short poem* and *Poetry Salzburg Review,* where some of these poems first appeared or will soon appear. An earlier version of one poem was published in *In Daylight* (Printed Matter Press, 1995).

CONTENTS

I *News of the World*

The Blue Edge	9
Beach	11
Poseokjeong Bower	12
Ginseng Wine with Mr Kwon	13
Watching the World Lightweight Boxing Championship on TV While Eating Dinner in a Bulgogi Restaurant in Kyongju with Chirone	14
Three Stone Buddhas	15
How to Paint the World	16
Pak Wayan, Sitting on the Veranda of His Losmen	18
The Waves	
Over the Mountains	19
In the Village	21
Some Roads in Bali	25
Kubutambahan	26
Mount Batur	28
A Dance in Ubud	29
Hall of Justice	30
Borobudur	31
A Courtyard in Bangli	35

II *On Arrival*

On Arrival	39
Straw Against the Winter	43
Zazen for Foreigners	46
All That Flows	48
In Izu	49
Mountain Road	51

Glimpsing the Garden   52
Sanjūsangen-dō   54
Four Postcards from Kyoto
    Saihō-ji   56
    Philosopher's Walk   57
    Nanzen-ji   58
    Ryōan-ji   59
Climbing, Descending   60
Deep in the Night   64

III *Current Accounts*

Habitat   67
The Real Thing   67
Perestroika   68
Guinness Book of Records   68
Capitalism in the Eighties   69
Supper in Houston   69
The Albanian Deprivation   70
Marketisation   70
A Slight Misunderstanding of the Nature
    of Democracy in the Friday Sermon 71
Hit List   71
Live from Cairo   73

IV *In the World*

In the World   75
Hotel Bangkok   77
Gold Rush   79
Ceremony at Ayers Rock   80

Notes   85

I

news of the world

for Chirone

THE BLUE EDGE

Moalboal, Philippines

1

from the beach you can see it
the line where the sea turns
from turquoise to cobalt
from coastal shelf to deep-sea trench

in facemask and snorkel we
swim out through shallows
gliding just above
a coral garden in full bloom

ochre brains bulbous on the seabed
pink branching vein-like intricacies
orange many-throated sponges
lavender-blue lungs draped over boulders

2

suddenly we reach the edge
a precipice where
the seabed drops away and we're left
hanging above

an abyss, into which
the imagination plummets –
that's much too deep! –
(the crush of millions of tons of blue…)

fish flit over the edge, silver sparks
vanishing
into depths beyond
daylight's reach or our cognisance

3

night
heavy limbs and sunburnt shoulders
salty tangled hair –
we lie in darkness, drifting

just above the surface of sleep
half-awake to
the *shooosh* of the sea beyond
the palm-frond walls, that will repeat

all night without our hearing it
as we float away from shore, suspended
above our own dark
unsounded places

BEACH

mounting towers of boiling cumulus
processional
above the hills of Negros

but not going far
burning off before they can cross the water
to this white beach where
the sky's been blue for days

sun-blaze
ripples lisp on hot sand
hermit crabs scuttle or stay interminably still

I sit with barely a thought
in the shade of a palm-frond shelter

the sea breathes its colours
a peacock walking in the garden of the world
turning its feathers this way and that way
coruscating in the sunlight

never the same glint or flourish twice

        no blueprint
        no schedule

there's no such thing as chaos

POSEOKJEONG BOWER

Kyongju, South Korea

among pine trees
a dusty stone channel
raised a little above the level of the earth

where, on summer nights, poems
and cups of wine
were floated down with the current

until one evening the future arrived
uninvited
and a king fell on his sword

the stream still flows
its water now
too low to feed the sinuous granite channel

the palace gone, paddy fields surround
this accidental monument –
an epigram in

undulant curves of stone
on the themes of power, pleasure
and their passing

a trinket fallen
from a dynasty's pocket
in tall grass beside a country road

Mr Kwon
in his white shorts
with his shock of short black hair and his glasses awry

Mr Kwon
with his sudden pronouncements
his outbursts of total merriment
his fierce one-thing-at-a-time concentration
his treatment of all people alike
and his perfect impatience with all linguistic impedimenta

fills my glass with ginseng wine
and gives me a piece of calligraphy, a Korean song, he says

what does it mean? I ask

he adjusts his glasses and sits up very straight:

Mongols come Chinese come man goes man fights woman cries Japanese come man goes maybe dies woman cries many wars Korea many wars Americans come communists come many wars now 38-line country divide man gone maybe dead woman cries this means this song very sad song please sing

WATCHING THE WORLD LIGHTWEIGHT BOXING CHAMPIONSHIP ON TV WHILE EATING DINNER IN A BULGOGI RESTAURANT IN KYONGJU WITH CHIRONE

marinated beef sizzles over charcoal
the table is spread with reds and yellows and whites
an anthology of kimchi in small ceramic bowls

cross-cuts, zoom-ins and close-ups
            bloodied faces
                        rivulets of sweat
assault and battery orchestrated
            into three-minute episodes –
short, sharp variations on the theme of harm

            for *human* read *male,* says Chirone

as one of the fighters hits the canvas with a wallop
            and stays there
the referee crouched and counting
the audience screaming –
            and then the winner's glove is raised

next up:
the weather forecast

we raise our glasses in a toast to
            several hundred miles of rain-filled cloud
last night's warm front
now moving quietly across northeast China

THREE STONE BUDDHAS

weathered
      smudged with green lichen
sitting out the centuries
under pine trees in a walled enclosure

      soldiers in chain mail deploy
      among blossoming trees

last night in pelting darkness
rainwater drenched their heads and laps,
      sluiced off carved stone bases
into the loamy earth

      a peasant woman stoops
      in stifling heat to light a stick of incense

this morning, steam rises
      from warming branches, sunlight
dapples the statues' granular repose

      an ant carries a yellow
      leaf across a carpet of pine needles

three stone Buddhas
      sitting out the centuries
under pine trees in a walled enclosure

      snow grows like white moss
      all through a winter night

HOW TO PAINT THE WORLD

Kubutambahan, Bali

a tree-lined strip of tarmac threads
the life of the northern coast on its string

every inch of the canvas should be filled, the figures embedded
almost to the point of disappearance among the frieze of leaf,
plant and tree

children burst out of houses by the roadside,
hallo, hallo, big grins, hands held out towards
us (palms vertical, fingers splayed)

let the painting be like the forest in all its anarchic orderliness,
where everything is decentred – or, if there is a figure at or near
the centre, a maiden, for example

three laughing women carry steadily sections of
bamboo balanced steadily on their heads along
a grassy path through trees

or a warrior

in the roadside barracks young boys with shears
clip the commandant's lawn, sentries lounge
with sub-machine guns

even then the detail of the rest of the painting should not be
reduced to 'background' but should exist in its own prolific
integrity

dogs, chickens, ducks, grey piglets with spines
so curved that their bellies almost drag along the
ground

and the 'central' figure should be depicted merely as a figure that
happens to be in the middle and not as any kind of centripetal
or radiating presence

schoolboys in white shirts, their names embroi-
dered on their breast pockets in blue, wait by
the roadside for the afternoon bus home to their
village

PAK WAYAN, SITTING ON THE VERANDA OF HIS LOSMEN

we cannot afford politics, we must all work for
the country, for the growth of the country

1965

when we have developed the country, then maybe we
can have politics, but as for now
political parties are a danger, they divide the country

80,000 dead in Bali alone

but we debate, we take part in meetings, in
discussions, but they are always
to put a road in here, to dig a new well there

villages, rice fields, ditches, lanes, rivers

no politics, if you speak politics, they
will kill you just like that, I have seen it, and
it is right, no politics, first we must develop the country

'small rivers and streams literally clogged with bodies'

THE WAVES

1 *Over the Mountains*

the minibus blares through
     a green world of palm tree
     banyan bamboo frangipani
swerves, horn blipping and braying, around
     ox-carts parked jeeps,
     stopped bemos skittering bikes
races below fields on steeply terraced hillsides
     (green rice yellow rice –
     two or three crops a year)
twists up into the mountains
     (mosses shrubs trees and grasses
     banked green whorls of fern)
bowls northwards through the uplands
     (eastwards, blue volcanoes
     rise into pearly cloud)
descends to Singaraja
     (dim tree-lined streets slope
     gently through the town to the sea)
barrels along an avenue of ancient trees
     (broad whitewash sashes
     painted around their waists)
and drops us at
a palm- and bamboo-sheltered beach

...

bright-painted outrigger canoes
hauled up in a ragged line

failing light
slate-grey evening sea

    cumulonimbus heaped
    high on the horizon

        the day's last patch of blue
        streaked with wisps of cirrus

small waves
flop onto black volcanic sand

    *

2 *In the Village*

a palm-fibre rope
        suspended
                from a line of planted sticks
leads out from the shore, supports

a net
whose upper edge is further buoyed
        by bobbing floats, made
from old cracked rubber sandals (everything is useful)

the fisherman
                sits all day
in a shady palm-frond shelter on the beach

wades out from time to time
                                along the line
a triangular bamboo-framed scoop-net in his hand

...

a man in a straw hat
guides a heavy wooden plough drawn by two fat
brown oxen that
        heave, themselves, through, the,

squelching, stubborn, thick, brown, mud

...

the look-out waits under his leafy roof

when a flock of birds
arrives to pillage the rice, he
agitates the web of threads
        that radiate from his shack
                out across the fields, triggering a

        rattle and a clatter of
        dangling tin cans –

the flock explodes upwards and away

…

in paddy fields after planting
ducks feed all day on insects, snails and weeds

dabbling, paddling, aerating the water,
fertilising the fields with their droppings

until at sunset the duck-herds bring them
back along the beach to the village

fifty or sixty in each flock, all moving
as fast as their legs will carry them, necks

thrust forward all at the same intent angle
(a regiment of small fat men running through mud)

being 'driven' (although they know the way)
by a lad carrying

a wavering bamboo pole with a
white rag

lolling at the end of it

...

sunset tonight
huge cave of ragged fire

...

torrential rain in pitch darkness
        reverberant thunderclaps
rainwater pours from thatch
sheet lightning momentarily
                illuminates the rice paddies

        silhouetted palm-trees
        gesticulate against the sky

dancing pencils of electricity
teeter on the jet-black sea

...

this temperate morning
        a man climbs a palm tree:
rope twisted in a figure-of-eight supports his feet
his hands grip the trunk
a machete is stuck in the belt of his shorts

the machete sounds
        high in the tree's bushy head
coconuts rain down, hit
the ground hard and heavy, and
bound across the grass

and then two or three
        brittle swathes of spiky leafage
crash down through the warm, still air, as
on the beach

the waves

make small lapping noises on the sand

SOME ROADS IN BALI

a quiet road past paddy fields
a road that dips between earthen banks
a long, straight road lined with trees
a meeting of three roads in a patch of forest

a grassy track that leads to a straggling village
a sandy lane that leads towards the sound of ocean
a green-hedged defile
an open road beneath an enormous sky

a road that climbs the volcano's shoulder
a pot-holed road between low buildings
a dark road lined with shuttered shops
a road out of a village, moon high above the trees

KUBUTAMBAHAN

1

steep steps ascend
    from a grassy terrace
to a stone platform with an empty throne

      (a sitting place for a god
      absent just now on heavenly business)

carved reliefs throng walls and balustrades:
    flowers, tendrils, maidens and warriors, gods –
and mustachioed demons
with vast nostrils and apoplectic eyeballs

who lean towards us out of the stone,
yellow lichen growing quietly over their faces

2

back on the street
we sit on a wobbly roadside bench
beside a small shop selling
fruit, rice, baskets, bottles, sandals and soap

women chat, babies balanced on their hips
children squat to eat spiced soup
piglets forage among rickety food stalls
a dog sleeps in the dust

across the street a frangipani sheds
a petal or two into a stone-lined pond
half-choked with lilies and lotus plants
and sheeted with rich green scum

      the world is
      particular and perfect

a bus pulls up, a passenger
alights and offers
flowers
in a small palm-leaf tray at the temple gate

MOUNT BATUR

Pine trees in grey mist, damp
jets of roadside fern, cloud-wrapped
houses with corrugated roofs strung out
along an ancient volcano's rim – and then

the weather clears: a caldera
ten miles across, a grey-blue lake
curled against its inner flank, and an up-
thrust cindery cone rising at its centre

to three raw craters: ribbed mouths
stained with chemicals, fissures
in the habitable world of bamboo,
buffalo, rice-plant, ant, and egret,

where village women, serried
offerings of fruit and flowers
balanced on their heads, descend
with grace the path to the shrine,

where rice fields step deftly down
a green staircase of terraces towards
the volcano's farthest reach – the barren,
boulder-strewn skirt of ash and gravel

which twenty years ago came
fanning down – incandescent and
ungovernable – from the gaping
(and, just for now, quiescent) vents.

syntax of elbow and wrist
talkative fingers
punctuation by glance and raised eyebrow

knees flex
exact swift placings of the feet
as though the dancer were

floating, were only deigning to
touch foot to floor
at the music's instigation

to humour it, to honour it
to point up its
effortlessly orchestrated syncopation

or as a favour to
the dignified seated musicians
whose mallets ding

on xylophones and gongs
(a consort of ringing treble
and groundswell bass),

who shift tempos without missing
a beat, their accents
jolting the staring-eyed dancer into

shiverings, abruptly poised stillness
and sudden
avalanches of gold-glittering movement

HALL OF JUSTICE

We gaze up at the painted ceiling
in the ultimate court of appeal
of the vanished kingdom of Klungkung –

the afterlife illustrated, an
encyclopaedia of the fates awaiting
unrepentant malefactors:

rape, dismemberment, attack by dogs,
assault with knives, clubs or spears,
ingestion by fiery-tongued dragons,

or bisection of the skull by
dreadlocked demons wielding
double-handed saws with great élan.

Be Good Or Look What You'll Get!
is what the ceiling tries to say, but if
once it worked, it doesn't any more –

the artist spared no pains to represent
the last word in atrocity, but we today
can view his images almost with affection,

as marvellous naiveties, because
we know by now that hell is only ever
here on earth, is made by men, and is not

the visitation of any conceivable justice.

BOROBUDUR

1

an iron bridge across a torrential river
shanty-shops beside the path
cold drinks and Buddha statuettes
baseball caps with peaks inscribed BOROBODUR

world mountain
        glimpsed through palm trees
a great beached vessel of grey volcanic stone

2

corridors thronged with carved reliefs
kings, queens, princes, courtiers
soldiers, servants, commoners, priests and hermits
cows, carts, ships, markets, temples, elephants
asuras, bodhisattvas, kinnaras, gandharvas and apsaras

        (the graceful tribhanga pose:
                flexed neck and hips,
        one leg relaxed, the other
                supports the body's weight)

carved narratives of
the Buddha's previous incarnations
and His most recent life

nine clockwise spirals through the galleries
to reach the highest terrace

3

ranks of stone figures –
        the Buddhas of the four directions –
sit, gaze out over palm tree and rice field
to blue mountains wavering in distant haze

        on the fifth terrace, Vairochana,
        the Buddha of the zenith, instructs:

right palm raised and facing outwards
thumb and first finger joined in a circle

4

terrace after grey stone terrace
a forest of iconography that has weathered
invasion, insurrection, the fall of kingdoms
earthquakes, eruptions, iconoclasts' hammers
tropical rain and the smother of jungle

designed by Gunadharma (ninth century)
using ratios of calendrical significance

        (the recent stone-by-stone restoration
        a seven-year, three-dimensional,
        two-hundred-thousand-ton jigsaw)

inhabited by no incarnate or commanding power
        a dance of carved stone above the abyss
        a mathematical flower of the void

5

the upper terraces are circular
no carvings
silent stone beneath blazing sun
an assembly of hollow bell-shaped stupas

peer through
diamond-shaped gaps
in lattice-work stone too hot to touch

        inside: Vajradhara
        the transcendent Buddha

hands poised in
circling dynamism, turning
the wheel of the law

6

A bus party of Muslim schoolgirls arrives, clad in the
headscarves and long skirts of the Islamic revival. They
laugh and chatter and take photos of each other as they
climb from level to level: it's a fun day out. One lingers,
then finds herself separated from her group. A small frown
puckers her brow as she looks around and hesitates – as
though perhaps noticing that, just within earshot, music
in a different key and at a different tempo from what she's
used to is being played.

(Many of the Buddha statues have been vandalised, their heads knocked off by iconoclasts.)

The other girls can be heard talking and laughing one level up, while she stands, caught in this moment of doubt and introspection: a small face framed by a coloured hijab, an anxious teen among the stone waves of iconography. Then she bethinks herself, makes some internal adjustment to her spiritual dress, and runs quickly up the steps to re-join her sisters.

7

at last the
uppermost stupa
on its lotus base

capped by a flat-topped
hexagonal spire
about 25 feet high

nothing inside it

empty and perfect

ceramic tiles beneath bare feet

whitewashed walls

an intermittent breeze

a small flag on a bending roof-top pole

bamboo wind chimes dangle

random pentatonic notes

drop

from a deep blue sky

hear it

the invisible world of the wind

II

on arrival (Japan notebook 1981–1982)

ON ARRIVAL

city lights glitter
        from horizon to horizon
the plane descends

stainless steel slatted ceiling
immaculate high-sheen floor

notes and coins
come across the counter in a little plastic tray

oh, right!
in Japan *first floor* means ground floor

...

plastic-wrapped slippers
tissues in a 'leather' container
disposable razor, disposable toothbrush
shower cap, clothes brush, shoe horn, emergency torch

        everything in its place

a slot machine sells magazines in the lobby
the green tea dispenser dispenses green tea in the corridor

...

narrow streets
printing presses in wooden shops

an ornamental lake, stepping stones and carp
a gravel path between dark trees

outside the subway station
        a just-under-life-size
smiling plastic statue of Colonel Sanders

...

in the underground concourse, a
cascade of commuters pours
        over the lip of the staircase
filling the passage from wall to wall

        no sound but

the shuffle and flap of
shoe-soles on polished floor

...

deep winding valleys
            north-west of the city
sombre with ranked cedars

the bus rounds a curve:
concrete, turbines, transformers and sluice gates

pylons head off
in easy strides over mountains in four directions

a small rain-wet graveyard
holds its own by the grassy verge

...

stone tank at the top of wet stone steps
rinse the mouth
bow, toss two coins in the slatted box
clap twice to call the god's attention

a deep drum booms among shadowy pines

...

to customs at the airport
to collect unaccompanied baggage

I've forgotten to bring the keys

one of the lads
from Nippon Express
        picks the lock of my trunk:
we are purofesshionaru

        . . .

two-ring gas-range
tile-floored bathroom
        (wooden bucket and re-heatable tub)
six-mat living room
balcony with a reputed view of Mount Fuji

in the local shopping area:
        pink tinsel street hangings
and a loudspeaker on every lamp post

        . . .

bookstore in Shinjuku
transcriptions of Ainu oral literature (whales and bears)

a sudden awareness of being in TOKYO
thirty million people, all consuming

Tokyo & Chichibu, 16–29 September 1981

among pine trees
stepping-stones bedded in moss

a sliding door
a garden glimpsed –
        grass, rocks, shrubs and gravel
wooden pillars, creamy plaster, grey tile roof
an open door, a seated monk half-seen

the drone of a chanted Sutra floats
        thinly through chilly air
from time to time the monk
twitches the shoulder of his garment straight

        deep note of a bell

yellow, red, or brilliant orange leaves
shiver down
        to cold dry crusty earth
to fade in brittle grey-brown heaps

a thread of white water spills
from rock ledge to rippling pool

. . .

wind rushes through
tree tops, thrums
in power lines and pylons

thickets of bamboo
swirl, bushy heads
dishevelled by the wind

footfall on trodden earth,
a sudden hush
in this pine grove, sheltered by

a cliff, where an eroding
sandstone Jizō sits, red-bibbed,
in his carved niche beside the path

...

a stone tank fed by
a trickle from a bamboo pipe

      a tin cup with a bamboo handle
      rests on the chiselled rim

the temple bell hangs from its beam,
      two tons of silence
dense with centuries of reverberation

gardeners crouch, hands working fast
      beside shuttered wooden buildings,
planting bulbs in loamy earth

the trunks of the trees
already wrapped
in straw against the winter

Kamakura, 21–22 November 1981

with Nishijima-sensei

instructions for posture

> *you need not think anything*
> *you need not feel anything*
> *just by sitting we*
> *penetrate to the foundation of the Buddha's teachings*

(pause)

are there any questions?

after zazen a lecture:

the Buddha's four philosophies
can be equated (in terms of Western philosophical logic) thus:

1. *agony*	=	*idealism (thought/intellect)*
2. *aggregation*	=	*materialism (feeling/senses)*
3. *action/non-consciousness*	=	*realism/existentialism*
4. *reality*	=	*reality itself: <u>not</u> philosophy*

he writes the word DIREKTIC on the blackboard

Hegel's dialectic encompasses
the first three philosophies but remains theory
realise the fourth philosophy (reality), and then the first three
                                                            become

        extremely clear

sitting in quietness only

the Buddha realised the splendid world

I can say yes and no at the same time

Tokyo, 6 February 1982

a tunnel cut through stone that leads to
a corridor of vermilion torii that leads to
a sunlit hollow among wooded cliffs

> ferns, a pool, a waterfall
> a red bridge to a diminutive shrine
> a cast-iron incense-pot, from which
> smoke coils up in slanting sunlight

in a dark cave
water ripples from a spring, flows
through stone tanks where, it's said, washing
your money will double it

candles flicker
bells dangle from coloured streamers

> eggs offered on altars,
> an image of a woman-headed snake:
> Benten (Sarasvati) – goddess of
> music, water, time, and eloquence

pellucid tones
of flute and koto
spill softly from speakers at the tea-house door

Kamakura, 11 *February* 1982

massed boats, coiled ropes, heaped nets
mooring lines quiver and plash
the sea runs fiercely, clambers
sandstone cliffs in sheets of spray

at the inn, fish in teriyaki sauce,
hot saké and half a crab each
brought to us by
Mrs Watanabe in her cheerful apron

...

clear morning
a high winding path with sudden views down to
blue sea
curdling to white around rocks

grey canted roofs tucked into narrow valleys
(scales on a cubist snake)
fishing boats in inlets
undulating loops of floating buoys

pine-logs for growing mushrooms
are stacked beside the path, slivers of
rust-red bark
scattered on the forest floor

the dirt track descends through
woods to the village, where
in terraced fields
edged with yellow straw

fat, white-domed
green-tufted daikon protrude
six inches above
Mr Watanabe's black and finely sifted soil

Dogashima, 20–21 *March* 1982

MOUNTAIN ROAD

sunset:
the yellow digger rests
its knuckle on the ground

Izu, 21 *March* 1982

GLIMPSING THE GARDEN

tea ceremony at Kennin-ji

green-and-white rectangular cakes
yellow confections shaped like birds

shaved wooden spikes to eat them
    (bark left on at the upper end)

overlapping gold clouds swirl
    on a black lacquer tea caddy
whose lid is removed to reveal:

    an astonishment of green powdered tea

the cup is placed before you : bow
move it to one side : bow : to the other side : bow
raise it : rotate it : take a sip

deliciously bitter, rich in texture

    the pattern in the glaze begins to
    gleam through green froth
    as the tea is drunk

meanwhile, intermittent
    slight rearrangements of
objects around the charcoal hearth

    (attention!)

sliding screens are
                        shot open for a
glimpse of garden then shot closed again

Kyoto, 4 April 1982

SANJŪSANGEN-DŌ

(the thirty-three-niche hall)

inside the 120-metre-long
        shed-like building
(exterior wooden walls almost black)

the spirit of thunder
        (eyeballs, muscles, torso,
        dumb-bells, a whirling circle of drums)
and the spirit of the winds
        (snout, tusks, knotted scarf,
        a bulging bag athwart his shoulders)

and then the twenty-eight guardians, who carry
wheels swords bells drums bows arrows flutes and lutes,
their heads circled with haloes of fire

and one hundred rows of gold-leaf bodhisattvas
each face crowned with
        ten more faces inside a spiky halo

and at the centre of all this
the bodhisattva of compassion
        (carved by Tankei – *at his late age of* 82)
sits on a golden lotus
saving numberless worlds with her rippling forest of arms

a priest in black, green and white vestments
recites a sutra and dings his bell

        preserve me, I pray, from all obstacles
        for the sake of all sentient beings

smoke spirals from incense bowls

a candle flickers in the gloom
to the fleeting honour of Kannon

Kyoto, 5 April 1982

FOUR POSTCARDS FROM KYOTO

Saihō-ji

stones
        embedded in moss
water slips
        between banks of moss
under lichened trees
                the glow of moss
over dark water a footbridge
                        smothered in moss

faintly, from the temple hall
a chanted sutra, the
thum thum thum thum, exactly regular, of a drum

        donnggg! of a large bronze bell

two old men sweep leaves

...

Philosopher's Walk

dark evening at the canal-side
        (blossoming trees and floating petals)
an old man surrounded by
                a scrum of firemen
in fire-resistant suits and silver helmets

        the old man narrates, with
        shocked, unhappy gestures

the firemen prod with sticks
the smouldering skeleton of a yakitori stall
interrogate with their flashlights
        each blackened cranny
of what was, until ten minutes ago, a livelihood

        ...

Nanzen-ji

painted golden screens:

a tiger prowls beneath green splashes of bamboo
a tiger leaps, extends a ripple of tail
a red-tongued tiger laps at a swirl of water
a whirlpool of curled-up tiger sleeps and dreams

the shōji are open
the wooden veranda looks out on
a miniature ocean with its scaled-down archipelago

      stones
                  moss
                            raked sand
          and clipped pines

behind the temple
      a red-brick aqueduct:
slick black water sluices between dank trees

...

Ryōan-ji

fifteen rocks sunk in five
pools of green-brown moss

Kyoto, 5–8 April 1982

CLIMBING, DESCENDING

breakfast at six a.m.
in a hut on
a saddle between two peaks

      pink dawn-light,
            mother-of-pearl mist
      swirls up from the valley

out: traverse a snow-field, ascend
a boulder-filled gully and then a spur –
      dangling chains and
      steel ladders bolted to rock –

to the scarp above, where
      a low, matted carpet of gnarled
fir-like bushes hugs the stony ground

      gloves on, a piercing wind

razorback ridges
      no clean rock face anywhere
everything broken, spiky, splintered
a precipitous wasteland
      mottled with snow patches,
furrowed and streaked with snow-filled gullies

      mist from the valleys
      licks and curls at the peaks

a cornice
(impressive even in its springtime dotage)
beetles over a snowfield

finally! sit in eddying cloud on the summit –
blue sky in patches, peaks
appear, disappear in mist –
brew coffee, sip from the finger-warming mug

in the silence
of high mountains
beep of an electronic watch

...

wake at five a.m. in the range's highest hut

muted dawn-light, keen
wind across the snow-field

traverse to a broken ridge

swallows' wings whistle as
they curve and skim above snow

toil across scree to a boulder terrace

snow smudges in
north-facing crannies

drop down into the valley's curve

> *trees bigger as the path descends*
> *the river bit by bit noisier*

pine-needles, red-barked pine trunks

> *'mountains & water'*
> *a traveller in a landscape scroll*

the river tumbles in its stony bed

> *jump, skip, boulder to*
> *white rounded boulder*

a level way among trees

> *turbulent*
> *confluence of ice-cold waters*

wildflowers beside the path

> *walking the grass of paradise*
> *in a sweat-soaked shirt*

valley lodge

> *a pinewood corridor to*
> *an eight-mat room*

framed in the window:

yesterday's peak
high above the trees

Kamikochi, 3–4 July 1982

banks
porno-cinemas
pachinko parlours

> *in the mountain village*
> *the wind rustles the leaves*

the river
flows, channelled by concrete,
        between the backs of office blocks,
reflects the silver street lights

street crossings
        tweet or cuckoo from
loudspeakers bolted to lamp-posts

> *deep in the night, the deer*
> *cry out beyond the edge of dreams*

Nagoya, 2 October 1982

III

current accounts 1989–1991

Habitat

from the top of Tokyo's highest building
on a clear day

7% of the world's GNP

The Real Thing

Aristotle Onassis's

barstools
upholstered in genuine

whale scrotum

Perestroika

bought these old battle tanks
from a new company over there in Leningrad

we have an option on a further 3,000 tons

it's good scrap metal
heavy and compact

Guinness Book of Records

Michael Milken
F. Ross Johnson
Charnoy Thipyasa

    $550 million
    $53.8 million
    141,078 years

      salary
      golden handshake
      imprisonment for fraud

Capitalism in the Eighties

we just couldn't
keep our hands off of it

Supper in Houston

140 cooks working for four days

3 ½ tons of brisket, sausage, chicken, ribs
1 ½ tons of coleslaw, potato salad, beans
1,250 gallons of barbecue sauce, pickles, jalapenos
500 pounds of onions
5,000 servings of cobblers, carrot cake
650 gallons of lemonade, iced tea

six guests

ostrich boots, a 10-gallon hat, and a mandolin
for each one
as a mark of the President's respect

The Albanian Deprivation

we're leaving our country
because we don't like the communists

we are young

we are poor

we've never even seen a
discotheque

Marketisation

in keeping with our commitment
to customer choice, you will pay
only for the air
you actually use

should you exercise your right
not to breathe at all
there will be no charge other than
the meter rental fee

A Slight Misunderstanding of the Nature
of Democracy in the Friday Sermon

if you don't vote for
the Islamic Salvation Front
you'll go to hell

Hit List

artists beauticians civil servants
doctors hairdressers
intellectuals lawyers
sellers of French newspapers
teachers writers
young women who wear immodest clothing

      bullet in the brain
      decapitation
      evisceration
      the severing of limbs and genitals
      the slitting of the throat

although we cannot – of course – condone such killings
we should remember that such people are not innocent

well Bob the spirit here seems to be very supportive certainly all the people I've spoken to both here and earlier in the day when I went out for a walk in the streets seemed pleased that Saddam is going to be taken down a notch and are very glad that finally this thing has at last got started and seem very elated by the early successes of the allied air power although of course this mood is to a certain extent fragile and we must remember that after the United States Egypt has the greatest deployment of troops in the theater that is about 40,000 in Saudi and another 5,000 in the Emirates and that there has been no ground action as yet and I think that once that ground action starts that if several thousand Egyptians are sent home in in in are sent home in er are sent home er

(dead)

I think that then the mood may change very rapidly and it would be difficult to maintain the initial enthusiasm and of course another factor is

17 *January* 1991

IV

in the world

IN THE WORLD

heaps of rubble
manholes without covers
open drains
uselessly set piles of cement

trishaws, tuk-tuks and buses
two-stroke engines and car horns
street vendors selling
bootleg cassettes and single cigarettes

shops warehouses workshops
shutters raised
metal sheets and hanks of steel cable
bales bundles boxes crates and cartons

piles of planking and girders
disembowelled jeeps
the flash and sizzle of spot-welders
repair shops spilling onto the street

air-conditioned banks guarded by
men in tight trousers, handcuffs
and truncheons dangling
from polished leather belts

as night falls
in every shack
the flickering light of the TV screen –
American heroes, Japanese anime

or soft-spoken generals in spotless uniforms
speaking of duty
speaking of family, speaking of
the safety of the nation

a child plays in the dust
in the light that spills from the doorway

HOTEL BANGKOK

on the brightly lit sign in the street:

> ringleted hair, a halo of flowers
> and the legend PARADISE FOR EVERYONE

in the ground-floor coffee shop:

> young Asian women in halter tops
> and fat pink men in shorts drinking beer

in the lobby:

> backpackers (residua of a previous incarnation
> of this address as a travellers' junction)
> checking their guide books

all these somehow less substantial than

> the miasmic reminders of the Founding,
> the wraiths of amphetamined GIs
> drifting in swathes along stark corridors
> seeking connection connection as you walk to
> > your room

three layers in twenty years
an archaeology of atmospheres and economies

the key unlocks the door
> to a bare utilitarian room
with a message from The Management
stencilled on the mirror

No Smoking In Bed

of which some previous occupant
assiduously with a razor blade
has scraped away the first five letters

GOLD RUSH

Mariposa, California

trail
camp
claim

tent city
saloon
whorehouse

murder a nightly occurrence

courthouse
jail
church

Indians negroes and mulattoes
may not testify against a white man
although they may testify against each other

town clock
hotel
railroad

closure of whorehouse

highway
Hollywood
chamber of commerce

TV

gifte shoppe

CEREMONY AT AYERS ROCK

I

the Anangu people
        prefer you not to climb it
they also don't call it that

        (some white premier of South Australia)

for them, climbing the rock
        has only one fit occasion:
the opening of the men's initiation rites

                to ascend the sacred path
                to point a camera at the landscape?

the lens should be focused within

2

a thousand feet up on the bare red sandstone summit
a dawn wind shivering
across hundreds of miles of scratchy bush

snakes, wallabies, ghost gums, desert oaks
honey ants, lizards, spinifex, caterpillars, grubs

3

after the descent

walking in red dust below the massive sandstone shoulder
glimpse from a distance the initiation sites
partly masked by trees

no photographs please
even to stare is sacrilegious

4

the light plane heaves and slithers through
the furnace breath of desert updraughts
crawls towards then circles high above Kata Tjuta

      huge lion paws of red conglomerate
      reposing in the pointillist bush

then turns and trembles back towards Uluru

I press the shutter button
(a new film loaded for this occasion)

      a click, an electronic whirr as
      the camera winds the unexposed film
      irretrievably back into its cassette

5

the plane lands
we unbuckle and clamber down the steps

after the climb has been completed
ensuing actions
whether dancing, walking or doing chores
are incorporated into the ritual and become sacred

dusty earth
walking barefoot, feel it hot between the toes

and this continues until the end of the ceremony

notes

NOTES

PAGE 18: Wayan is a name often given to the eldest sibling in a Balinese family; Pak (literally, 'father') is an honorific. 'Losmen': an inn or hostel. The last line is from an article about the Indonesian massacres of 1965 in *Time*, 17 December 1965.

PAGE 44: Jizō (or Ojizō-sama, to use the respectful form) is the bodhisattva Kṣitigarbha, protector of travellers and children; small statues of him (often wearing a red bib) are frequently found beside roads and paths in Japan.

PAGE 64: The lines in italics are from a poem by the eleventh-century poet Minamoto no Morotada included in the *Shin Kokin Wakashū*, the eighth imperial anthology (1205).

www.ingramcontent.com/pod-product-compliance
Lightning Source LLC
Chambersburg PA
CBHW031208090426
42736CB00009B/828